SEVERE WEATHER

HURRICANES

BY BRIENNA ROSSITER

WWW.APEXEDITIONS.COM

Copyright © 2023 by Apex Editions, Mendota Heights, MN 55120. All rights reserved. No part of this book may be reproduced or utilized in any form or by any means without written permission from the publisher.

Apex is distributed by North Star Editions:
sales@northstareditions.com | 888-417-0195

Produced for Apex by Red Line Editorial.

Photographs ©: Shutterstock Images, cover, 4–5, 8–9, 10–11, 18–19, 22–23; GSFC/NASA, 1, 12, 13, 15; Bernandino Hernandez/AP Images, 6–7; Neal Dorst/OAR/AOML/HRD/NOAA, 14; Lieut. Commander Mark Moran/NOAA, 16–17; Harry Koundakjian/AP Images, 20–21; Robin Lam/SCMP/Newscom, 21; JSC/NASA, 24–25; iStockphoto, 26, 29; Kristen Lemoine/USDA Natural Resources Conservation Service/USGS, 27

Library of Congress Control Number: 2022901429

ISBN
978-1-63738-304-9 (hardcover)
978-1-63738-340-7 (paperback)
978-1-63738-409-1 (ebook pdf)
978-1-63738-376-6 (hosted ebook)

Printed in the United States of America
Mankato, MN
082022

NOTE TO PARENTS AND EDUCATORS

Apex books are designed to build literacy skills in striving readers. Exciting, high-interest content attracts and holds readers' attention. The text is carefully leveled to allow students to achieve success quickly. Additional features, such as bolded glossary words for difficult terms, help build comprehension.

CHAPTER 1
A STRONG STORM 4

CHAPTER 2
HOW HURRICANES FORM 10

CHAPTER 3
DANGER AND DAMAGE 16

CHAPTER 4
STAYING SAFE 22

COMPREHENSION QUESTIONS • 28
GLOSSARY • 30
TO LEARN MORE • 31
ABOUT THE AUTHOR • 31
INDEX • 32

CHAPTER 1

A STRONG STORM

A hurricane hits a coastal city. The storm's strong winds pull up trees. They fling cars. Heavy rain pounds the ground.

Powerful wind is one of the most dangerous parts of a hurricane.

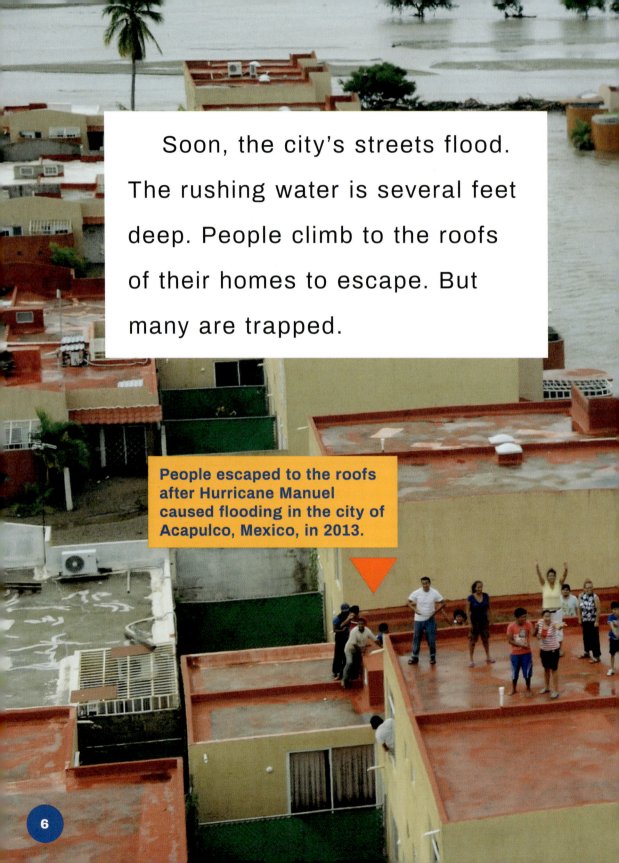

Soon, the city's streets flood. The rushing water is several feet deep. People climb to the roofs of their homes to escape. But many are trapped.

People escaped to the roofs after Hurricane Manuel caused flooding in the city of Acapulco, Mexico, in 2013.

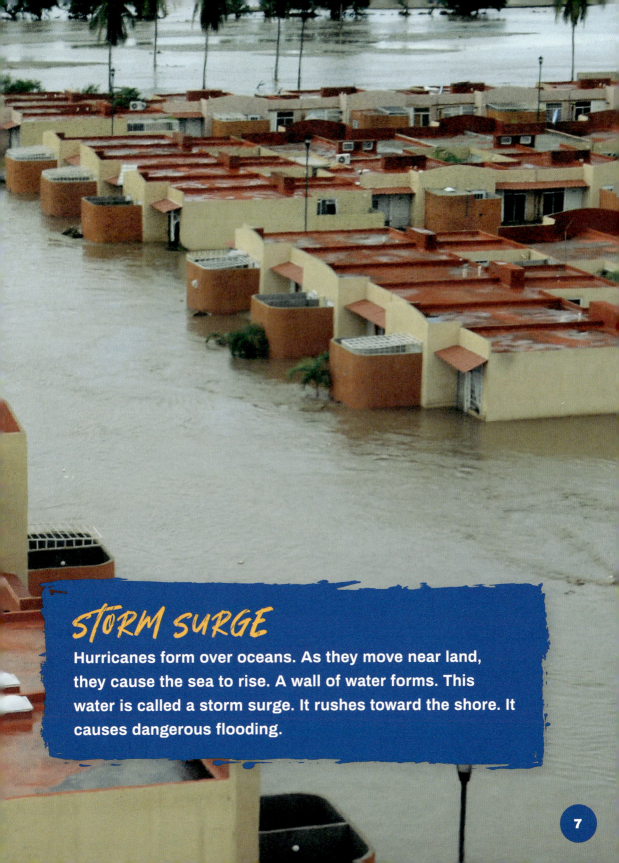

STORM SURGE

Hurricanes form over oceans. As they move near land, they cause the sea to rise. A wall of water forms. This water is called a storm surge. It rushes toward the shore. It causes dangerous flooding.

The storm lasts several days. Many buildings are destroyed. The city will take months to rebuild.

In 2018, Hurricane Michael destroyed many homes in Mexico Beach, Florida.

Fast Fact

Some hurricanes cause **mudslides**. They can wash away whole towns.

CHAPTER 2

HOW HURRICANES FORM

A hurricane is a large storm with fast winds. Warm air rises from the ocean. It cools and forms clouds. More warm air rushes up after it.

Ocean water temperatures must be above 80 degrees Fahrenheit (27°C) for hurricanes to form.

Storms in the southern half of the globe spin clockwise. Storms in the north spin the opposite way.

The moving air makes the clouds spin and grow. If the wind reaches 74 miles per hour (119 km/h), the storm becomes a hurricane.

Around the world, dozens of hurricanes happen every year.

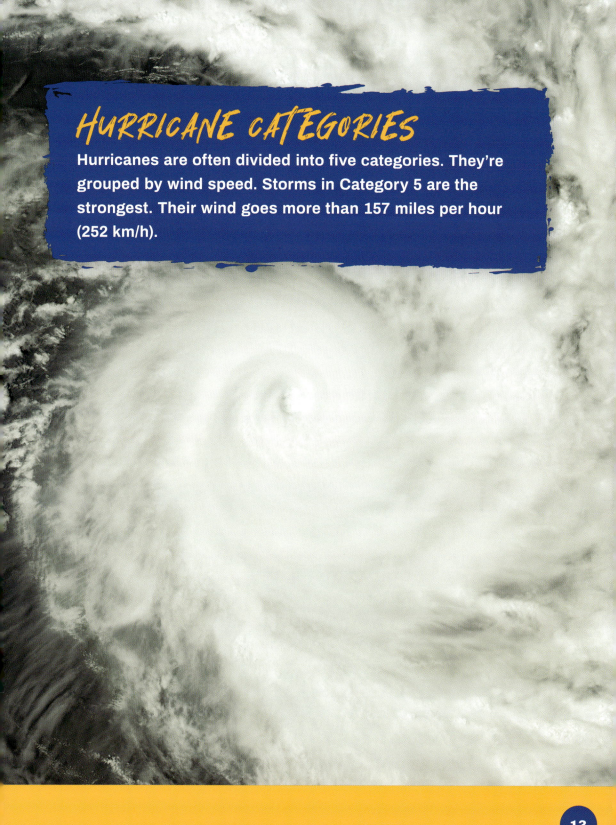

HURRICANE CATEGORIES

Hurricanes are often divided into five categories. They're grouped by wind speed. Storms in Category 5 are the strongest. Their wind goes more than 157 miles per hour (252 km/h).

A hurricane has three main parts. The eye is the calm area in the middle. Tall clouds called the eyewall surround it. **Rainbands** spiral out farther.

A hurricane's eyewall has strong winds and heavy rain.

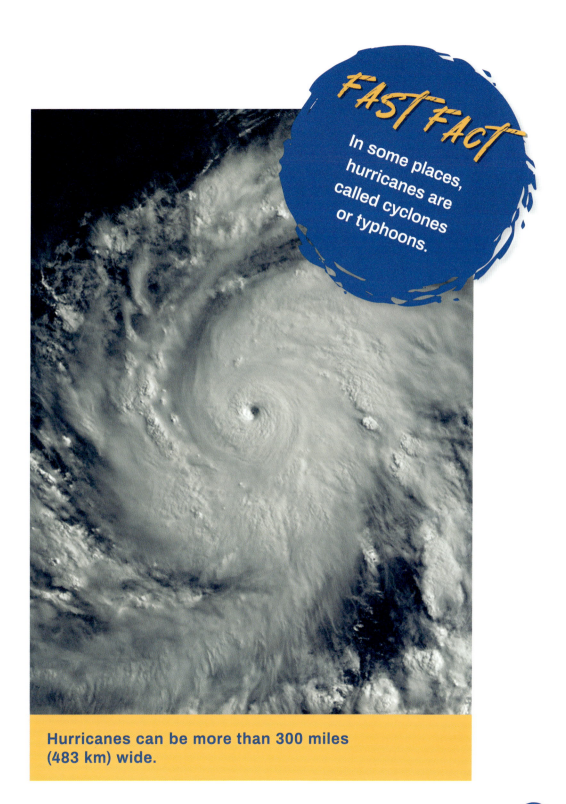

FAST FACT

In some places, hurricanes are called cyclones or typhoons.

Hurricanes can be more than 300 miles (483 km) wide.

CHAPTER 3

DANGER AND DAMAGE

Hurricanes are very dangerous. In 2005, Hurricane Katrina hit Louisiana. Much of New Orleans flooded. Thousands of people lost their homes.

At one point, Hurricane Katrina put 80 percent of New Orleans underwater. Some areas were never rebuilt.

Hurricane Maria hit Puerto Rico in 2017. Its fast winds made most of the island lose power.

Hurricane Maria's winds reached 175 miles per hour (281 km/h).

FAST FACT

A hurricane hit Galveston, Texas, in 1900. **Flash floods** reached all the way to Kansas and Oklahoma.

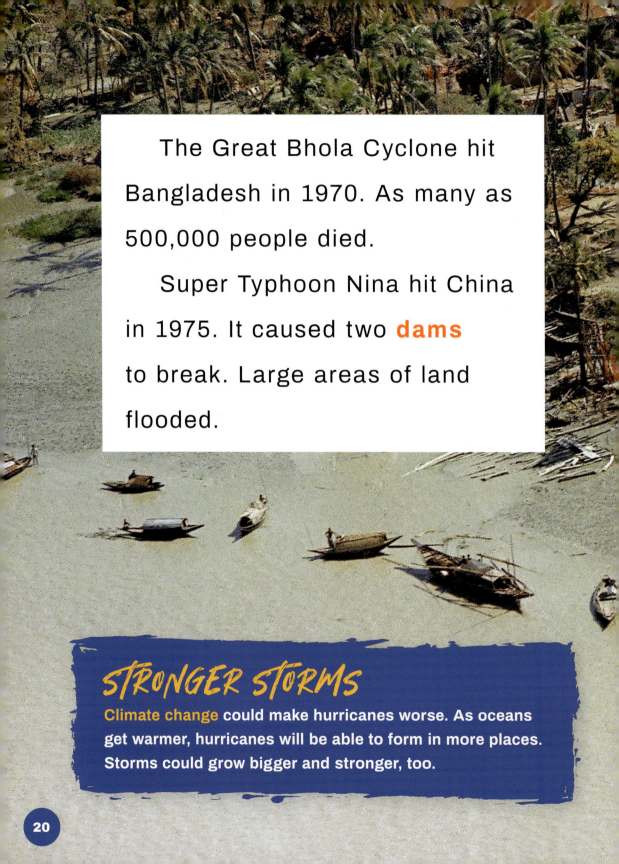

The Great Bhola Cyclone hit Bangladesh in 1970. As many as 500,000 people died.

Super Typhoon Nina hit China in 1975. It caused two **dams** to break. Large areas of land flooded.

STRONGER STORMS

Climate change could make hurricanes worse. As oceans get warmer, hurricanes will be able to form in more places. Storms could grow bigger and stronger, too.

The Great Bhola Cyclone was one of the deadliest storms ever.

Super Typhoon Nina's winds reached 115 miles per hour (185 km/h). Many buildings were destroyed.

CHAPTER 4

STAYING SAFE

People prepare for hurricanes in many ways. Some places build **levees** and **seawalls**. These structures hold back water. They help stop floods. People also design buildings to survive strong winds.

Seawalls can help make storm surges less harmful.

FAST FACT
Some airplanes fly in or near hurricanes to study them.

Scientists track hurricanes. They use computers and **satellites**. These tools show each storm's speed and location. They can also help tell where the storm will go next.

Satellites and other spacecraft help scientists understand hurricanes better.

Scientists can warn people before the storm hits. That way, people have time to get to safety.

Before a hurricane, people often try to get far from coasts.

Between 1930 and 2020, Louisiana lost more than 2,000 square miles (5,180 sq km) of its coastal land.

NATURAL PROTECTION

Wetlands help prevent damage from floods and storms. Wetlands can slow waves and take in water. However, many wetlands near coasts are shrinking. Saving these areas can help people stay safe.

COMPREHENSION QUESTIONS

Write your answers on a separate piece of paper.

1. Write a few sentences explaining where and how hurricanes form.

2. Would you like to work as a scientist who studies and tracks hurricanes? Why or why not?

3. How fast must a storm's winds go for it to be a hurricane?

   A. 74 miles per hour (119 km/h)
   B. 157 miles per hour (252 km/h)
   C. 115 miles per hour (185 km/h)

4. How could heavy rain from a hurricane cause a dam to break?

   A. A dam can't work if water touches it.
   B. The rainwater could melt the dam's walls.
   C. The rainwater could crack or flow over the dam's walls.

5. What does **categories** mean in this book?

Hurricanes are often divided into five categories. They're grouped by wind speed.

   A. times of day
   B. levels of a house
   C. groups of similar things

6. What does **structures** mean in this book?

Some places build levees and seawalls. These structures hold back water.

   A. things that fall from the sky
   B. things that grow from the ground
   C. things that people make or build

Answer key on page 32.

GLOSSARY

climate change
A dangerous long-term change in Earth's temperature and weather patterns.

dams
Walls built across streams or rivers to hold back water.

flash floods
Sudden rushes of water caused by heavy rain.

levees
Walls built near rivers to stop water from overflowing.

mudslides
Times when huge amounts of mud fall quickly down hills.

rainbands
Clouds and storms that swirl out from a hurricane's eyewall.

satellites
Devices that circle Earth in space.

seawalls
Walls built on coasts to protect the land from ocean waves.

wetlands
Areas, such as swamps, where the ground is wet and soggy.

TO LEARN MORE

BOOKS

Adamson, Thomas K. *Hurricane Katrina*. Minneapolis: Bellwether Media, 2022.

London, Martha. *Hurricanes*. Minneapolis: Abdo Publishing, 2020.

Rathburn, Betsy. *Hurricanes*. Minneapolis: Bellwether Media, 2020.

ONLINE RESOURCES

Visit **www.apexeditions.com** to find links and resources related to this title.

ABOUT THE AUTHOR

Brienna Rossiter is a writer and editor who lives in Minnesota.

INDEX

C
Category 5, 13
cyclones, 15, 20

E
eye, 14
eyewall, 14

G
Galveston, Texas, 19
Great Bhola Cyclone, 20

H
Hurricane Katrina, 16
Hurricane Maria, 18

L
levees, 22

R
rainbands, 14

S
seawalls, 22
storm surge, 7
Super Typhoon Nina, 20

T
typhoons, 15, 20

ANSWER KEY:
1. Answers will vary; 2. Answers will vary; 3. A; 4. C; 5. C; 6. C